Walnut Wednesday

The Book

"I have witnessed my own personal evolution from Peanut Girl to Walnut Woman"

Lara Gieseke

Copyright © Walnut Wednesday 2021
Lara Gieseke
Wellington, New Zealand
All Rights Reserved
ISBN: 978-0-473-60350-2

Dedications

This book is dedicated to special angels

Heinrich und Leopoldine Gieseke
Karl Breiing
Daniel Ginty
Matthew Ellis

I also dedicate this book to Young Lazz, the younger version of me who aspired to publish a book but deep down never thought it possible. This is my gift you to, Little Lara.

Acknowledgements

with special thanks to

My father Horst Gieseke
My coach Rachel White
My friend Kate Bromley

I also acknowledge the support from
my partner Jordan, my sister Clarice (Rick),
my family, my friends, The Walnut Tree collective,
my mentor and friend Viola Hug and the
teachings and readings with Amy Melissa

Foreword

by Rachel White

This book is a work of true art, a mosaic of broken and seemingly random pieces that have come together in a way that only Lara could arrange.

Lara embodies what it means to be a 'walnut' – a term she coined, that means to be a person who decides to be brave. It is her decision to step into her own bravery that has already activated inner bravery in people around the world. Lara is someone who leads by example and allows others to witness her throughout her journey (a rare combination in the world), I remember the first time I asked her to be on my podcast a little while back now and she was 'scarecitied' (a term you will read more about as you turn the pages) but she decided to be brave and now she has spoken on so many podcasts and other places. This is only one example of how Lara's brave actions ripple into more magic in the world. Lara is a woman who has a lot of stories to tell because of the action she decides to take. Writing this book is a further extension of her bravery and I am incredibly grateful and honoured that I got to work with her as her coach in bringing this masterpiece to life and into your hands.

This book is a big permission slip for everyone who reads it to pave your own path, create works of art however the fuck you want to, and to choose to be brave even when you also feel scared.

Prelude

A Facebook Post from September 2019

My Story.
How did I get here?

In September 2019, I took an online programme about starting your own soul aligned business, hosted by Psychic Expansion Coach, Viola Hug. I really had no idea what I was getting myself into, other than the feelings of being scared and excited at the same time.

I guess a good start is to begin with the statement that I have always known and felt that I am different, and that I have always felt an amicable sense of separation from people around me. For example, I grew up the only Sagittarius in a house full of Gemini and growing up (even now, actually), I never really had a group. I believe the term is "social butterfly" although I don't remember high school being as free and glorious as that term sounds. I sort of floated and hopped, coming into new friend groups (all of which knew each other from early ages) and situations, but never actually falling into a place that I myself was a part of from the beginning. I had a very "normal" upbringing and was lucky enough to have not only nurturing parents but also grew up basically living with my grandparents - just that little bit of extra love, there is no more special cuddle than an Oma (Grandma) cuddle!

I am half German and half Filipino. The Grandparents that were part of my upbringing, were from the German side. The first language I spoke was German, so I grew up bilingual. I have a memory of bike riding with my Opa Karl to the dairy - I would have been around 6 - and a man commented on Opa Karl's bike (it was an ancient old thing) and little Lara stepped in explaining that he could not speak English and stood there translating for the two men about a bike from English to German and back to English. It was so natural to me; however, in school I was very embarrassed that I was "other" to everyone else; because my grandparents spoke very little to no English, when I would have to speak in German in-front of people I would feel absolutely mortified.

I am ashamed and completely the opposite now! In fact, I would give anything to be able to sit across the table from them and chit chat in German, over Kaffee und Torte (coffee and cake) once more.

When I was little my interests consisted of: fairies, crystals, loving animals, playing with my Oma's necklaces, eating Kartoffel und Butter (potato and butter) and, of course, putting on theatrical shows in my back garden. To be honest, I am pretty sure it was just me swinging around a tree like the little monkey I was, but hey, it was a show, okay! The people who attended my shows: my sister/co-performer, grandparents, parents and occasionally the neighbours referred to me as the "show off" or "chatter box". My dad always talks about my first overseas trip to Fiji, where I would have been about seven years old. As you're walking through the resort with me, you'd hear a "Hi Lara!" and my replying "Hey so and so" (even adults!) from people that I had met on my adventures; charismatically just being lil ol' me, cruising around my Kids Club and the resort just doing my thing.

*

One of my first run ins with death was when our dog, Gusti, died. She got kicked by horse living in the horse paddock at the end of our dead-end street, and had a heart attack. We buried Gusti in the same garden where my hit performances were born and I remember walking back up to the house, on our narrow footpath by the light of the moon and felt a compelling need to kneel, throw my crystal up in the air (I had left it with Gusti's body and dad gave it back to me before we put her in the ground) to the moon and bow my head. What the actual fuck, I hear you ask? Yeah, me too... but at the time it just came over me and I did it. I don't even remember what I was thinking, just that I wanted to. My mum asked me what I was doing, kind of freaked out as anyone would be and told me to go inside. That was the first and only time that I can recall, where I have ever impulsively done something where I did not know what came over me or why.

Deaths after that took more common grief journeys - no crystals to the moon included. The words "killed himself" came into my world around Form 2 (also known as Intermediate School) and then later, throughout High School the word "suicide" popped up indirectly, with people I knew; which was a strange and hard thing for me to comprehend. How could you be laughing immaturely through a drama class with someone and then discover they died and you didn't notice something was wrong?

At the time, high school felt like the end of the world, but I finished it going through all the usual trials and tribulations of your typical teenager: "where do I fit in", thinking I was fat (and now it's like that meme, I wish I was as fat as the first time I thought I was fat), feeling like no one understands, thinking I am ugly, feeling alone, self-mutilating, experimenting with booze and all the things, boys, discovering girls can be so MEAN, the list goes on. The fairies, love and theatrical shows dwindled out and turned into heavy metal, dragons (although I always had dragons, they just went from colourful to slate and grey) and trying to hide in the background but simultaneously wanting to be different and be noticed.

During this time, I took my first dip into Personal Development and made the choice to see a counsellor. At first it was a finding-myself-show-off attempt to skip class with a friend, pretend we were depressed (secretly I think we both were, in a teenage hormonal angst kind of way) but later found it was more than that. I continued to regularly show up (I think during a Mean Girls saga) discussing why people are the way they are, what is in it for them or for me and how to deal with issues that did not originate as mine, yet directly affected me. I believe I really discovered my sense of self early through this. I remember one morning, in the first class of the day rambling out some philosophical 'woowoo' to a friend about life and she groaned rolling her eyes telling me it was too early to be so deep. I smile as I write it now, but at the time I felt so segregated, like some old lady in a 13-year old's body. I am only just now coming to accept my sensitivity and empathy as a strength, whereas then, I felt so weak and I took great comfort in discussing these issues with my counsellor.

I would later be back in counselling, not for coping mechanisms to survive a Mean Girl saga, but again with the intention of other people's issues and develop ways in which I could help them. August 2012 was the start of a pivotal shift in my life, where everything I ever knew in the months to come turned upside down. I don't really know how to describe this shift in me, because it was neither positive, nor negative, but after over year (all of 2013 I actually cannot remember) in shock, I would call this change, something like waking up or coming into awareness. It was, to be put simply, noticing what was important, noticing that it wasn't all about me and it was me, discovering a type of strength I didn't know I had. I had to learn, on my own, yet in a pack, how to survive being left behind.

August 2012 was the first time I was directly affected by suicide and four months thereafter, in December 2012 the same yet different piece of my heart broke, a second time. Two of my very best friends were gone.

The conspiracy, the why, the others affected are not a part of this story, nor mine to tell, but what shaped me was how I kept on living. I didn't tell myself little affirmations about how my dead friends would want me to be living or living in the name of; for a while there it was dark, black and it was all about me. I didn't understand how the world kept going, when all you want is for it to stop. I was living in a sombre cloud of nostalgia and I did not leave this space for a long time. There came a point however, where my internal differentness shone its little head inside my bubble of sleet, where I started my philosophical internal observations and I decided, this shouldn't be how things were anymore. I had to look after myself so that I could try and look after my circle. The people in my foresight needed something and I did not know how to help them. So, I went back to counselling, discussing why people are the way they are, what is in it for them or for me and how to deal with issues that did not originate as mine, yet directly affected me.

Now, this all sounds very saintly but it was all a bit of an internal battle where all I wanted was to feel helpful. This actually led to years of people pleasing and a very empty cup (only something I have recently got on top of). It was never for any kind of recognition or praise; I just have this innate need inside me to try and help. You will always see me trying to give advice, sometimes when it is not asked for... or trying to support a small business, I just can't help it! Now I know it's part of my Human Design - shout out to my 5/1 profiles - we can't save everyone OK!? Don't get me wrong though, I have had my fair share of being a far-king biiiiiiiitccchh - a bully even!

Which leads me into my most recent awakening, or rather a big, stinking slap in the damn face. I woke up - oh man - I'm finding this hard to write, even though I know I don't have to share this if I don't want to. I hate myself.

There I said it. I've been doing a lot of reflecting on things I have said and done over the years and... I don't really like who I am. I feel ashamed, I feel uncomfortable, I feel mean and weak. I imagine who I used to be vs where I want to be and see confidence but here in the middle, I just feel stuck and self-conscious. This is what brought me here, discovering that some of these things are actually my strengths, like my empathy. I'm diving into why I am the way I am, what's in it for me and everyone else and how to deal with issues that are 100% mine and have been affecting me silently for years.

I am still the cheeky little monkey who performs theatrical masterpieces on a daily basis, I still love the high pitch squeal of Danny Filth and I most certainly still love potatoes AND butter.
One of my final conversations with my counsellor was where I made the statement "I am just trying to find my place in the world" - so here I am, still trying. I have a loving family, an awesome long-term relationship, a most wonderful collection of friends and I have so so much love to give, but it needs to start with me, Lara Marie Gieseke. I need to love myself first and I am so excited. Wish me luck!

Walnut

(noun)

A person who decides to be brave.

I want to preface that this book is a real-life account of moments in my life, my trials, my learnings and my special moments.

What you're about to read is a snippet into the life of someone who thought that they were here to just be, for someone else, everyone else, anyone else; who would never really *be* a lighthouse but wished and deep down and somehow *just knew* that they could make an impact on the world. If you learn anything from this book, Walnut, it is that, if a little small-town girl can take a simple picture with a Walnut in-front of her face and in doing so, shed so many internal, personal ideas of who she thought she needed to be; then you can too! You can move mountains if that is what you desire. You can change the world, your own world, just by walnutting, deciding to be brave even, as little as just the once a week.

You will notice that the chapters of this journey are fittingly linked to podcast episodes where I have practiced my voice to explain these moments, these lessons and findings. I encourage you to listen to the episodes mentioned to complete the expression of my story with your experience here, within my words. You will have space to share your thoughts, if you wish to, below each episode mentioned and do not feel afraid the express yourself in the spare spaces to follow within this book – you are worth it and you will not ruin the page. This book is yours; your thoughts are yours and my journey is for you to listen and read alongside in hopes that you too, will resonate with being a braver, walnuttier version of yourself for years to come.

I'm going to start my journey here, from where I'm sitting. I'm sitting at the old dining room table in what was formerly my grandparents' house, now my parents'. I'm sitting at the corner in a small spot of sun, listening to our Fat Birds chirp. My late Opa Karl called the birds his children and was always feeding them food left overs and stale bread. Needless to say, his legacy lives on and, his children have since become inhabitants of this Raumati residence evolving into little - and by little, I mean to say, plump - round balls with feathers! I'm sitting on an entirely different end of the spectrum than where I was at the beginning of 2020, the year of big things. I knew deep in my heart, without it being the "new year new me" cliché' that 2020 really *was* going to be *my* year... and oh what an awakening it was...

I've recently learned that in order to hold the power of a high, you equally need to understand and accept the lows. In hindsight it is simple to see those lows, slowly creeping in to suck you dry; but when you're living on the surface of a high, right when things are seemingly great, to me it feels like a huge slap in the face and a huge shock to the system. Let's start this story there, where I, as I'm sure you've similarly been, decided it was time to leave a job that was no longer serving me.

scarecited [scare-cited]

(adjective)

When a person experiences feelings of scarcity and excitedness, at the same time.

Admittedly and in typical Lazz fashion, it took a good, few whacks to the ol' self-esteem to really declare this decision to the universe, let alone say it to *someone* out loud. It scared me because as pressured as I was, I was comfortable and I made things work around that comfort. My work/life balance was all consuming to one side and, admittedly, the word that described it was certainly not "balance", especially on a mental level. I settled. I was settling. I'd been stubborn trying to make it work to the point of burnout. I know now, in hindsight, that I needed to be there, that long, for five years, so that I could experience a state of strange, foreign, delicious, empowered, walnutty confidence that it took walking out with my head held high.

Now, only months prior I'd had practice at this. I'd been registered with a gym that was, in all honestly, quite cult-like; you know the ones, Walnut, everyone wants to be friends and high-five and GO ON HIKES IN THEIR SPARE TIME, TOGETHER?! If it isn't obvious, Walnut, I don't people and I especially do not people at 6am while I'm sweaty and my breath, despite brushing my teeth, smells like last week's sewage dump! Seriously... who wants to make hanging out plans, that early, that sweaty and that peopley? People at that gym, that's who! Walnut I digress, but as I paint this picture, let it be known that I really did enjoy the high intensity training at this gym. I didn't have to think, I didn't have to speak to anyone if I didn't want to, they had good music and a variety of different routines each day – which satisfied my open-heart centre and my sacral in Human Design, immensely.

The walnut story is that there are usually two coaches for each class, who go around and rah rah you, tell you, you can do it and sometimes pick on you to kick your ass and get a good workout in. Well, one day, I was changing up an exercise, which was very common for me because I have odd, bung knees that don't like heavy impact from running or jumping and a coach came over, noticed I wasn't doing the correct one and picked on me a little bit. Over the music, I sort of mouthed that it was my knees and as the coach left my little area, I saw both coaches make eye contact and the other rolled her eyes.

Now, it was one of those polarising moments where you either know it was about you or, you need to reality check yourself for being paranoid and *making it* all about you. Either way, it was in my mind about me and in that moment, I decided I was not paying "huge" amounts of money each week to be made to feel that small; like I was a burden, that I was worth nothing short of an eye-roll for something that is genetically an issue.

We need to back track a little bit to my morals and values at the time, Walnut, because while they haven't changed all that much, my morals and values to myself, have. I was always a person that resonated with loyalty to a fault. Yes, in the past I've done things that contradict this, but all and all, I was a person that stuck with things, stuck up for things and justified my moral compass on a scale of loyalty. I was reliable. To the detriment of my own wellbeing, if you needed me, I would drop everything for you. It's sad really, when I think about this person, because I really took pride in how loyal I really was. I remember I'd planned a retreat for work and as a team bonding and discussion exercise, we had to choose if we resonated with gold or steel and explain why. All the gals chose gold, because it looks nice, it's boujey and it can be formed to make the most beautiful of things. Me? Well me, Walnut, I chose steel, because it is strong, it doesn't need the bells and whistles and after everything, it is a strong foundation that will not faulter. Steel will always be there. It sounds beautiful as I think of it now, but in my mind back then, I really didn't think I was *worthy* of being gold, of being shiny and being seen. I saw myself as a key foundational piece in other people's stories and I genuinely didn't think I needed or wanted to shine. A huge shift from the young girl swinging around singing and performing from an apple tree with a forced audience, right?

So, after a time of this kind of self-resentment, being at the job I was in included, I walnutted. After that eyeroll and in that moment, I took my values on loyalty, the belief that I was special for being a foundational member and I shoved it up my own butt. I had nothing to prove to any of these people by staying within this membership and I especially, after all the little stories I told myself was not going to be made to feel like I'm an issue, worthy of an eyeroll that early, that sweaty and that people at 0600am in the damn morning! I terminated my membership that day and that small spec of empowerment was only the beginning. This, was the practice round, a little piece of evidence under my belt and in preparation of the test to my worthiness and self-esteem that I was yet to encounter.

Misguided Loyalty

Walnut Wednesday the Podcast episode #5

"I do not deserve this! - I am loyal to *myself*"

When I truly started to voice, out loud, that the role I was in was affecting my self-esteem, I knew from the bottom of my heart, that I needed a change. As I mentioned, loyalty being a value that I still hold close to my heart was, during this time, infused with stubbornness and fear. I didn't want to let anyone down, I wanted to make it work and I wanted to create a success story while I was there, to leave some kind of legacy where I would be remembered as a foundation piece – like the idea I had of steel - at this job. I was also scared. Being a creature of comfort and routine for so long, I was so unsure of what the outside world would bring. This job was my home, my cocoon, my first real-life-grown-up role; an "International Travel Consultant" I was a professional and a party gal at her finest. In the peak of her mid-twenties who worked hard and played hard (a motto that circled the company often) with an ever-changing team and many bonds made in-between.

During this time, I was genuinely challenged with using my voice. I'd had many a confronting conversation about my performance and for so long I thought there was something wrong with me. Only now, after a deeper look into my Human Design do I have the knowledge that that role was genuinely not for me and how I was deigned to live. The building relationships and the service, yes, but the competition, in a sales environment, the dangling carrot and the rah rah, not so much. I always took it so personal in these confronting conversations. I felt like I wasn't celebrated for what I was doing well and I was constantly asked how I can improve and to show specific action plans of where to do better. The constant moving target and monthly clean slate slowly chipped away at my self-esteem, not understanding that consistency doesn't actually work for my design, nor do specifics and nor did the constant pressure of an unrealistic number that I had to manifest into existence because someone said so and set the average.

I cried a lot near the end. I cried at the local café having a meeting with the big boss, I cried in the back to my Team Leader. I felt like the most sensitive sausage on the planet because I felt like my integrity and my values were constantly being criticised and at every single peacock parade, I could not help but roll my eyes and take it personally. I didn't believe in my company anymore. This was so hard for me to say at the time because it challenged every idea, I had of what 'loyal' meant. It was truly a rose-tinted glasses moment, where it felt like seeing the woods for the trees. I knew and strongly felt, that I deserved more than a dangling carrot peacock parade. A peacock parade, Walnut, and do not be offended if you enjoy these, are when the loudest, brightest, shining stars, with the funniest jokes and on the surface, seemingly confidence people show off their feathers and rah rah together. They might be your thing and if they are, go you! Because looking back now, the reason they were my worst nightmare, is because I always felt "less than" being there; so, chances are, if they're your thing, you're already at a place that took me five years to find!

The polarity was, Walnut, that despite the intense emotion about the back end of business and sales and the peacock, I really, truly loved my job. I loved the organising, I loved discussing new locations, the stories and reasons for travel. I loved packaging up ticket wallets, giving gifts and receiving little tokens of my client's thoughts from abroad. I received so many arrival gifts, which brought me so much joy (guess what my Love Language is) and I loved my clients so much – some of whom I still speak with to this day. So naturally, it pained me with the guilts every time I thought of applying something new.

Needless to say, my next move was certainly to physically do the damn thing and apply for something new. I needed to take the next step from declaring I was ready to leave and start to take some action. I feel like I am spending so much time here, Walnut, but you must understand, these few months were some of the most difficult of my life. It was a literal battle of the self, where I had to be brave and step into my worth and pushing against my stubborn engrained nature that there must be another way for me to leave a legacy here. It meant, a daily battle of guilt for wanting to leave and leaving, fear of the unknown, worry for my clients and trusting that they will get the same service when I am gone – the list, or rather the limiting stories I told myself, were endless – all despite enjoying what I was actually doing in my day-to-day.

I have to credit Walnut Wednesday here, because from following my gut and finding new walnuttings to share, I started to discover that the aspects of Walnut Wednesday that were morphing into a *movement* were lighting me up, like really sparking a fire up my butt and I was envisioning multiple versions of Future Lazz in the process. I really used this fire to fuel me through the impatience and rejections of still not being offered something new. The looming anticipation was not so looming when I put my focus into my new found passion project. I even I took it upon myself to create a live mini-series. Yup! I went live for five consecutive days; in a group I'd created but never invited anyone into (at that point) and taught from my experience – It was called "Walnut All Day – the mini-series" where I talked about five key things it takes to be a Walnut in my day-to-day life. I ran this, on an early morning, in the back office, before work, on my mobile phone, coffee in hand and I simply talked about myself. I really did have some expansive moments in that place and it's for those reasons and those relationships that I could never fault my time there. Looking back now, it all seems so divinely cultivated, you know, right place right time sort of thing. As if a little angel with a heart in the shape of a walnut was laying out my next move in complete confidence that I could do all the things.

On March 26th 2020 my life did a complete 360. I resigned in the blink of an eye. Over five years of my life gone. I'd been so restless since January, ready and waiting for the moment to resign, but when it finally hit, I didn't know how to process it. It was a (Walnut)Wednesday and I was accepted for a role to assist with COVID-19 calls, with an office close to my home (I don't think I mentioned my 2.5 hour commute every day to my travel job?) and immediate training for this job was with a start date of the Friday. I had two days to tidy up five years of my business as best I could. This moment, when I walnutted, decided to be brave and finally leave, was my lucky star, COVID-19 ironically gave me the "out" I was craving and I cried all the way (working from) home.

27 March 2020 – Facebook post
on the Walnut Wednesday Business Page

"WALNUT - tries not to cry (again)
I resigned today.

The universe has nudged at this for years and I never really listened until they became pushes.

Those pushes became shoves and all of a sudden, the universe smacked me on the butt and shoved a firework up me arse!

The country closes its boarders. Half our team get let go. The country goes into lockdown. I get a job offer. I resign and just like that I start a new chapter tomorrow.

I haven't said goodbye in person, I don't even have clothes that aren't uniform or active wear. I don't know what the eff is going on, I still feel like I'm in a movie.

"The universe likes speed" Oh yeah it bloody does.

Here's to the five years of growing, learning & the amazing collection of people along the way - especially my team.

Here's to a job I genuinely loved and wouldn't change for the world.
And here's to knowing this is right, that I'm celebrating and that I'm ready for it.

But also, someone get me another bourbon because I can't stop crying.

One of the last bottles of gifted bubbles, from a wonderful client, who I will miss with all my heart, all of them."

The Universe Likes Speed

Walnut Wednesday the Podcast episode #23

"I felt like I was just a number"

The moment I began to acknowledge and investigate why I didn't like myself, brought about a new knowing that I'd never felt before. In my time I've had many a 'courageous conversation' on a professional level, but the moment the need for one comes too close to home, I've avoided it. Usually, I'd stew and simmer and sweep it under the rug; you know, like a 'storm in a teapot' as my Dad would say.

If you hadn't guessed, Walnut, confrontation to me, is like hellfire. I despise it, my voice goes funny and because of how nervous I get, my body responds with bodily reactions like sweating, my throat closes in and all the words I've ever known fly out of my mind. I get all clammy and I feel weak when I am doing it and it is why I've always avoided it where possible – quite conceivably leading me to a life of people pleasing and feeling like a doormat for many, many years.

Along my Walnut journey, a trick I learned from my father, among the many talks we have, was a discussion on the metaphor "storm in a teapot". This was a total bird's eye moment where I was in the heat of emotion, having a vent at the dinner table, about a bad day and my Dad swooped in with an outside perspective, exhaled and said "storm in a teapot" – what the hell right? Here I am, expressing how angry I am in great detail. The snowball effect of every single example I could think of, to make my week seem more traumatic than a normal week, just to get my parents on side to sympathise, with the burden of anger that was immensely, all-consumingly bubbling up through my blood and coming out of my ears. All I wanted in response to my invitation of "that's annoying right?"

was some validation, telling me that those people are all bitches, that I am the king of the castle and that I should feel rightfully angry. And all I got was "storm in a teapot". LOL!

Now this response could have gone two ways. In the first instance, I could have shut the world off, added anger to this response and decided to feel like no one understands me. The second response - which was what I did – was that, in typical Line 1 Profile fashion, I got curious and asked what he meant. I decided in a moment that I was going to be emotionally intelligent, make myself vulnerable and potentially get shut down with a truth bomb. My Dad described it almost like a visualisation. Imagine you're in a teapot, the tea inside is hot, it's steaming, you're trapped in a whirlpool of tea! It's crowded, you're hot, you're sticky – you and all the things, all your feelings and turmoil are all just swirling around in there, right? Now, Walnut, read this in slow... motion... imagine just staring at a teapot... with hot tea in it. You might see some steam rising out... but other than that... it's just sat there... waiting... not affecting anyone... or anything. I KNOW RIGHT?! I know, it's all making sense now and I am sure, now you're thinking about a time that was totally *exhale* "storm in a teapot" aren't you?

If I am honest Walnut, my woes of that week consisted of, cryptic corporate guessing – the whole "is she mad at me" kind of thing – some small, immemorable things that I now don't remember and that I was also upset with my sister. Sibling arguments are worthy of a whole other chapter, right? And, in hindsight, they're somewhat refreshing when you have time to reflect on what was said. I do digress, Walnut, let's car park the family stuff! The point is, the list of my weekly vent was full of minute things. As I mentioned, I was even trying to *add* to the list with other petty examples to make my week seem more than, when ultimately, I was somewhat upset with my sister and I wanted my folks to feel sorry for me and especially, take my side. Family and in some cases, very close friends, are great for reality checks like this, aren't they Walnut?

One big learning I want to share from this experience is to genuinely check yourself, Walnut, and check where your feelings are coming from. Is it something you have to look deeper into? Is it a moment where you are choosing to simmer but you need that bird's eye view? It's hard to notice and it's hard to step into self-awareness and into the realm of choice, to decide to be brave by taking a look within yourself. Walnut, I take my hat off to you if you have or if you are doing this - because it's the looking that's the hard part.

Storm in a Teapot

Walnut Wednesday the Podcast episode #79

"If you imagine you're inside a teapot. You're in the storm and it's swirling around but if you're on the outside looking at a teapot, it doesn't effect anything"

It's funny Walnut, as soon as you start creating space and walnutting your way towards something, you come to understand just how much power you truly hold and are capable of holding. Sometimes, along the way things will creep up and smack you on the nose, sort of like turning 30. All of a sudden, your preferences change from pre-drinking a bott of sav in party girl stiletto heels with flames on them (yes, I still have these and yes, though collecting dust, I still adore these heels), to just drinking a bott of sav in your pyjamas at home, alone, with no obligation to speak to another human until the next morning.

Well, on this, let's call it an "aging transition" of my Walnut journey, another realisation was afoot and it was becoming palpably obvious where most of my conditioned behaviour was stemming from. Sometimes conditioning can feel so much a part of you, as much as the traits or habits it brings, can feel so foreign. It's like it's a part of you but you don't really understand why – like my former people pleasing tendencies – I know I have them, I know I've acted this way for a really long time, but where it stemmed from, I really did not know!

I was speaking with my sister-in-law about some family matters and she said something along the lines of "there comes a time when your parents become people, they're just doing their best". It's never really resonated with me until I really stopped to think about this more; and living back at home, with my folks right under my nose (or rather, me back under theirs), I noticed that *my parents are just people doing their best*. I noticed that my parents very possibly also struggle with fear, loss, stress and unworthiness – something you don't really *know* until you say it out loud, right? Parents are supposed to live on a pedestal, where they are higher, mightier and know all things; all until this "aging transition" where it's as if your brain just clicks into gear for the first time. I'm not talking about the age when your folks become your "friends", where you start to be able to have a drink with them and talk about grown up things; but a little further than that, where your parents become like aliens because in the blink of an eye, you realise "holy shit! You're just like me, trying your best and trying not go mad in the process!" ...wow!

It started to become abundantly clear that a lot of my shadow stems from how I've been raised, how my parents act and what they believe to be true. Realising your parents are just people is something that has brought up an emotional intelligence that I wasn't even aware I had, because, I can genuinely empathise with their situation now – is parenthood waiting for the kid to turn 30 for only then, them to realise this?! I can understand, now that I have given life a good crack, why they've acted certain ways, who they are as *people* and where this has filtered onto me.

In May of 2020, I went to bed in tears, feeling the need to write and wrote myself a long drunken 'chapter' you could say. I'd had a lot to drink and I'd had a lot to say and needed to express myself. It has been quite a long time since I'd felt called to write or draw and, in this state, it was interesting that I was coherent enough to even string a sentence together. Let's start from the beginning, Walnut, I'd arrived home late after a late shift and wanted to head upstairs to tell my Dad about the shift – which didn't often happen and especially not when I came home late. I noticed my Dad had been drinking and when I questioned him, he'd told me a (very) long story about how he was doing some work in the garden. He started telling me about what the dog was doing, the vegetables, what he intended to do while working down there – yeah, what's the point, Dad? As he came to the end of his story as to why he decided to have a drink he mentioned that he'd got so dizzy all of a sudden and the fleeting thought crossed his mind that if *anything happened* there would have been no one home, at least not for hours, to help. *I can* 100% say that I understood what my dad had said, without being able to put it into words. I could understand what it must feel like to want to do something that you can't, and that for years you could do which now tires you. I could understand that he felt shame and embarrassed for what he could not do, when others had done the same and more. I could understand that after that scare, he drank and drank until he couldn't pronounce Jethro Tull. And naturally, I joined him.

What hit me the most that evening was that I felt so confronted by my own father. I know now that it was simply realising he was *a person.* We played music from his past, most of which I enjoy, and when I suggested we play an artist that I too listen to, my Dad couldn't comprehend that I genuinely enjoyed the music, because it was his. It's all a bit of a 'storm in a teapot' now, Walnut, however, I'd finally had enough to drink that I decided to challenge this and my Father was incredibly defensive. It was in that moment I knew; I had triggered my own father and I knew, that this is where my conditioning on authenticity has come from. For whatever reason, I was *not allowed* or rather, he could not permit the thought of my genuinely enjoying this artist - not because my Dad had liked her first, nor because he ever knew I enjoyed her music. But because something was going on, and has been going on long before I was born, that challenged him on being unique. Where did this come from, this subconscious trigger from my Dad's past that it has trickled down and conditioned onto me?

I will never forget a conversation with my Father where he quoted an actor saying something about 'always knowing they were different'. This has resonated with me since I was young.

Never have I ever pulled my father off his pedestal and recognised that he too has triggers just like me. And never would I have I ever realised that they were something so personal to me. Authenticity, being "fake" and that I'm "just pretending" - you have no idea how much those words feel like fleshy battle wounds to me. Perhaps that is why I left the conversation feeling so upset. Because my "un-fakeness' was challenged, funnily enough by the exact conditioning that it came from? Was there something in particular that had happened to my father, that conditioned him to, in some ways, not be able to share experiences and deem it inauthentic when someone does? The funny thing is, Walnut, I know exactly why, because I've lived it. I've deemed it. I have looked at someone through squinted eyes, funnily enough over music, and declared their inauthenticity, their fake-ness, their *pretending*. Because it has been conditioned into me, yet I cannot give you words.

And because I cannot give words, here are some from Joni Mitchell...

Tears and fears and feeling proud
To say, "I love you" right out loud
Dreams and schemes and circus crowds
I've looked at life that way
Oh, but now old friends they're acting strange
And they shake their heads, they say I've changed
Well something's lost, but something's gained
In living every day
I've looked at life from both sides now
From win and lose and still somehow
It's life's illusions I recall
I really don't know life at all
It's life's illusions that I recall
I really don't know life
I really don't know life at all

When Parents Become People

Walnut Wednesday the Podcast episode #99

"Being a grown up, living with people who were the people who raised you, told you what to do, taught you how you think, as an adult now, with your own opinion, your own way of doing things, life lessons already learned; it does bring about a clash"

The saying goes "you can't choose your family" which also applies to in-laws, half siblings, you name it. Sometimes we are placed in situations where we don't get a choice with who sits at our table. However, and while the saying is true, I believe *you* can choose who *you* want to be in that family, as in, how you decide to behave and if you act with integrity or not.

I've had situations on my journey where I have felt so much disappointment, particularly with family, where I've really needed to walnut, be brave and stick to my morals and boundaries. Understanding that parents are just people or that siblings are just people or that every single person you've ever interacted with is *just a person* will bring so much more clarity as to how you behave and respond to situations.

God Speed, Walnut, because deciding to be a brave and be a walnut, in the beginning, is confronting, scary, heavy and lonely. Noticing things about yourself and the people around you will be shocking and at first and it is going to hurt. Sometimes a lot. I think the point I want to make with this chapter, Walnut, is that external things, like parents' validation, like flame heels, or even Joni Mitchell, will not make you whole and you're going to learn this very soon. Everything you need is inside yourself and you are capable of holding space for so much more of *you.*

Courageous Conversations

Walnut Wednesday the Podcast episode #85

"That is walnutting, to be brave enough to actually have those conversations and not let things slide, let them stew, let them snowball and let them get bigger and bigger until you just resent a person or, resent yourself"

The below section mentions suicide please do not feel pressured to read this chapter and skip ahead if you need to

Walnut, this is a chapter that I wanted to have inside this book, however, has been the hardest to write. It's a place that I do not like to re-visit often because the Big Black Wolf which will be mentioned shortly, is one I still carry and probably will all my life. I want to put a disclaimer on this chapter and encourage you to skip ahead if you need to. This chapter mentions suicide and my experience in losing someone(s) from it.

This chapter is important for me to share with you because of how much this experience and how much surviving being left behind has impacted Walnut Wednesday to its core. Though a place I do not wish to visit often; I still think this is an important walnutting piece that I want to share with you.

Walnut Wednesday is based on the basis of having courage and being brave and I believe one of the hardest, bravest things I've ever had to do was to keep on, after losing friends to suicide. In 2012 within the space of four months, two of my dear friends felt like the only way forward was to end their lives.

Sometimes grief hits you like a ton of bricks and other times it slowly creeps up on you in years to come, from a random way the sky looks to a certain lyric in a song.

22 August 2012 I remember looking for my friend. I remember thinking that this wasn't actually happening to us. This was what you heard about other people going through. I remember driving through our town, down familiar roads and I remember going to up to the cold hills and calling his name. All of us, with our hands curled around our mouths, to ensure the sound travelled far and wide. I will never forget, as four of us looked at each other, not wanting to say it, but all thinking the same thing. The moment where the phone rang and we got told to stop looking.
I'm not sure whose car I was in, or even who was driving but I remember Ben saying "You know what that means, right?" as we all sat silent in a car on the way to the home of our dear friend. I kept thinking of him all alone, wishing I could have been there. Though, if I could have been, what would I have really said?

I think when someone you know suddenly takes their own lives, the reason it is so hard to carry on is that it was a decision that *they* made. In my own selfish way, I personally was so hurt that I'd been left to carry this Wolf and it wasn't long before I had to carry it again. I worked for a director for a while. I would go to her house for dinner and we would talk about theatre shows. I'd be a stage hand for some rehearsals but mainly, we both had no idea what we wanted from each other and simply ended up talking, about her scripts most of the time. She was telling me a story she wanted to write, about carrying a black dog around that symbolised grief; which actually, as words, fittingly stuck with me in the years that followed. My grief *was* like carrying a black dog, only, for me, it was big, it was heavy, it was wild and it was a wolf from my pack.

It's like everyone can see it, but no one offers to carry it with you, in fact, people act differently because they can see your wolf and they don't want to feel uncomfortable by acknowledging it. The thing that will always get me with loss, Walnut, is how much it changes people, not only in your eyes but how some of the people closest to you can start to fade away. And he did.

As I am writing this, I can feel my shoulders tensing up, like I have two wolves on my back pressing me to share this next part. My visual is of someone that's been hunting, how one would carry a pig on their back, but on mine, I've two black wolves. I have to pause for a moment, to second guess if my mind is just me wanting someone to be there or if I can truly feel in my soul, that they want me to write this.

The four months that followed saw to my other friend hit his rock bottom. It was like watching someone spiral on a TV show but in real life and I will never forgive myself for never quite understanding - despite conversations that we both did. I never thought *he* would do it. Walnut, have you ever had "a person" and it's of a soul connection, not necessarily family or romantic? Well, this wolf was mine. He understood *it*. He understood me and situations that I was in because he'd been in them with me. It was a mutually agreed friendship where sometimes we didn't even need to speak to understand. But his wolf was getting too heavy and silly me, thought it was the same wolf that was eating at us all. In some ways his wolf pulled him deeper into the dark. He behaved strangely however, we were all in a shadowy cloud, I'd assumed this is what happens when you all carry wolves at once. Everyone carries in their own way, right?

08 December 2012 I got the phone call. He did hit rock bottom and he did it. How do you move when you get the news? How can you make the world stop for a second so you can catch up? I don't really know how I responded. I woke up Jordan and we got dressed but didn't know where to go. We moved but we weren't in our bodies. I made phone calls, on total auto pilot, not really registering what was going on. Everything changed. This was too close, there were so many factors and coincidences eternally bonding these wolves forever.

It was as if we had handled this before, we all knew what to do again. Sleep over at each other's houses, drink juice, tell people when it's okay to come over, answer questions to people who don't want to ask direct relatives. "I'm fine" when you're anything but. I'll never forget hearing his parents cry, early in the morning or crying myself to sleep or the last look he ever gave me – that cheeky little grin.

Some of this story is important I raise to you, Walnut, because, unknowingly to me at the time, my experience has shaped who I've become and has been a silent contributor to Walnut Wednesday all along. These wolves are the heart of my mission. I never, ever want anyone to feel so alone and like this is an option – or however I imagine my friends felt in their last moments. I truly believe that by stepping out of our shells, being brave and sharing or acting in what is vulnerable – walnutting - we can change the world. We can change our own world. We can change how we feel about ourselves and see us the way other people see us. Being a Walnut sets the standard of self-leadership, that if you're doing it then someone else can too.

The Elephant in the Room(s)

Walnut Wednesday the Podcast episode #41

"I think if you looked into my eyes back then, you'd have seen nothing behind them. I just moved but I didn't know I was moving. All you want is the world to stop so you can catch up, but you just never do"

I want to take you back to where I walnutted big, I had nothing to lose in regard to putting myself out there to be a Virtual Assistant. My needs were met on a human level, I had security, I had a new job and I had low living expenses. I saw one of my favourite coaches in the world advertise for a Virtual Assistant, with various skill sets required, but that training would be available and ideally, to be a Generator in Human Design. I thought in my mind I would not have a chance in hell, because of the list of technicals that were well outside of the basic systems that I use. However, despite having the thought, I was still pulled to send a message - something along the lines of, 'I'd require a lot of training, despite how well I can get things done'. She replied straight away asking me to email her my expression of interest with the systems I *do* know how to use. I remember feeling disheartened, while at the same time excited, perhaps another "scarecited" moment before I really had the feeling described. I felt like I wrote "would need training" over a hundred times, but I still carried on and wrote the most walnutty summary about myself at the end and I want to share it with you:

"I believe I can bring so much to the table and also see this
as an amazing opportunity for my own growth...
I would require some training, but once I'm there,
I will be a strong loyal foundation that will compliment your business.
You will know who you need on your team, but I felt pulled to reach out"

When I hit send it was like planting a seed of the universe and despite my need for training and lack of most of the technical skills, I was offered the job and, was told she'd be honoured to work with me! *cries happy tears*

I take you on this side story, Walnut, because you can see how much I love to serve. While yes, from the outside looking in, it looks like a great opportunity to have my foot inside the door of working online; note that all my roles up to this point are in service of others - which I am good at and, according to my Human Design (5/1 profile and left angle Incarnation Cross) my mission is inclusive of people and I do have innate tendencies to try and "save the day". This shows itself in many ways, sometimes it's simply referring a small business, sometimes it's going above and beyond for questions and sometimes, it is going to the ends of the earth to 'try and help' when *not* asked or wanted (I'm working on letting people run their own race). I am your perfect assistant, I'm organised, I'm loyal and in a work capacity I will churn through any tasks asked of me - I like what I do! If you are resonating with this, Walnut, I'd suggest you may also resonate with the idea of loneliness in some capacity too, as I do.

Let's talk about feeling lonely without actually being alone. The thing about the Walnut journey is there are parts that will be incredibly isolating, where you will feel a lack of support and incredibly stuck in the in-between.

At the time of my writing this book; I've felt like I am living a double life, with half of me in corporate and then other in an entrepreneurial fantasy, both of which I do not one hundred percent fit into. I think I can best describe this in many ways but the one that comes to mind is like a work best friend and then your childhood best friend. Sometimes, it just does not work to invite them to the same party – which is how I've felt with my new life as an Assistant, a Virtual Assistant, a podcast host and creator of Walnut Wednesday – essentially, three roles, or hats, as some would say, that I am ever trying to fuse together and I wonder when it will ever stop. My capacity for this works well, I am of course a Generator and most of my 'hats' do genuinely light me up in some way.

Putting myself out there for the roles that I am in now, have all been a step on the never-ending pathway, that is my life. Defined by choices, moments and who I decide to be. I've truly stepped into personal leadership with every step, which unfortunately means, at a point, we have to leave some things behind; and the journey to realising this, has been really tough at times. As I've grown, the people in my life have not necessarily grown with me and the people in my close support network, do not quite understand my 'double life'.

Many a friend I have had to leave behind and, in some ways, this was physical where we have 'broken up' or in others it was simply an energetic cord cutting, no bad blood, simply a difference in the way I exchange my energy. It's those moments close to home, though, Walnut, that have sometimes stung the most. Those small moments of sharing an idea and feeling deflated – you know, those moments when you're so excited and the moment you tell the wrong person it's as if you're a balloon and they've just stabbed a small pin, slowly into your side, so you gradually start to empty of the excitement you were carrying. That's not to say this was on purpose, Walnut, it is simply that our mission, is slightly different than what is considered normal, right? There have been times where I feel closer to the Walnuts I've met online in various containers, than my own family because they understand what I am going through, they're in the in-between too, just trying to be the successful versions of themselves in a capacity that isn't "the norm", just like me, with Walnut Wednesday.

It can be very tough in the in-between, Walnut, and my only advice to your craving support, if you are, if you're waiting for someone to be the air raising you up instead of the small subtle unintentional puncture; are two things. The first is to be brave, be intentional, Walnut, and have a courageous conversation. To me, this looked like a moment I had with my sister. I was so excited to share an idea with her, for one of my first paid, ever green offers. She told me that "it's a good idea but you should put it up on YouTube for free" and for the reasons below, Walnut, you can imagine this comment to me, translated to "you're embarrassing, you're not worthy of charging money for yourself and you suck". My response could have gone two ways, the first being crumble, keep the hurt and feel sad for a few days. However, what I chose to do was to explain to her how much that hurt my feelings. I said something along the lines of how important Walnut Wednesday is to me and sometimes when I am sharing an idea in excitement, I don't often want her advice, I only want to express my excitement; and I explained that when she gives me un-asked for advice, the way it comes out really hurts my feelings and deeply upsets me – I believe I was actually crying at the time of the messages because it just stung like anything. This boundary setting was received well by my Sissy, as they often are, when you are brave enough to speak your truth, and my sister gracefully explained that this was a world she didn't understand and of course, she'd never want to hurt me. We now have an alliance where, unless asked, she doesn't give me Walnut advice and I now have specific people I select to be a part of any idea-spinning processes.

Another way to build a support system, which is what I've had to do, links with the above boundary setting and it is to *look* around you at your collections of people. You may be surprised when you take the time to explore, just how much someone you've collected and decided to keep in your life may well be in the in-between alongside you. I had a moment like this with my best friend, Kate, who is a freelance producer. I was very upset at something I'd shared with someone close and felt like I'd been shot down from the little excited cloud I was daring to dream and fly on. She got it, she understood because her working hours do not look like that of 9-5, she doesn't have an office, she can work remote and manages her time and budgets accordingly to suit her non-linear lifestyle. This is the thing, Walnut, people are not deliberately trying to hurt you, even though in the moment it seems offensive and an attack. A main chunk of society only knows the 9-5 as the norm and anything outside of this is extremely foreign – I imagine like you starting your Walnut journey or trying something new. It's not wrong, it's just different and it does take looking at life from an alternate perspective to accept this. Choosing who you share your non-conventional things with is such a powerful exchange and once I'd cracked this code and was intentionally choosing who to ask for advice or share with, it truly did and continues to amplify the excitement; because someone gets "It" and can hold a space like that *with* you. It's like taking off your bra after a long day – you can relax knowing you are comfortable and you are safe.

Who Lights the Lighthouse?

Walnut Wednesday the Podcast episode #68

"I resonate with being a lighthouse and I guess I am tired of feeling like I am a light or the fixer"

I think one of the really hard truths in being a Walnut and beginning this journey is that is it not easy coming to terms with, or accepting the way other people are and no matter how much you wish you could, you will never be able to change that. I mentioned in the prelude of this book that I've constantly – and possibly from very early on – looked at why people are the way they are. I guess that's what I mean when I say "I've always felt different to others", even in a room full of people I love, I can still many times feel *alone*. I tend to look at things differently or feel things deeply and with age, in my "aging transition" I've come to be able to see behind, or rather, beneath the surface of some situations – why someone acts in a certain way, what made them do it – albeit with a slice of human, where sometimes my response is not the most intelligent and I'll quote Melanie Ann Layer here: "when emotions are high, intelligence is low".

I continue to learn time and time again that people are going to "do what they're going to do" no matter how much time you've spent trying to deflect or postpone the inevitable. The hardest part about this, Walnut, is that people are going to deeply disappoint you along the way (yourself included) and this has reared Bully Demon's little head for me in many ways over the years, each situation bringing about mass Imposter Syndrome of asking myself who the hell I think I am to think this way about the people I'm close to; especially when *I've* likely behaved this way all along.

I've had a fair bit of practice now about using my empowered 'no' and my aligned 'yes' and these examples, as always, come from the new found skill in boundary setting. If you haven't already, Walnut, I'd like to encourage you to reflect on where you have boundaries in your life. As a recovering people pleaser, I started by first looking at the places I was in and what made me, essentially, feel like shit. In hindsight it felt like the realisation just smacked me on the butt, but in actual fact, it was regularly shown this in the major resentment I was feeling, from constantly running around for everyone but myself.

One of the key pieces to boundary setting for me, Walnut, was taking a deeper look into my priorities and where I actually enjoyed spending my time. I noticed that I was flaking on experiences and people that I dearly love, that I conversate well with and ultimately, people who make my soul less hungry – is this what extroverts feel? I call these my "Sunshine and Rainbow Friends". I was choosing to prioritise different people, sometimes who had a little bit of drama going on in their lives, over people that genuinely wanted to spend their precious time with me for nothing other than the fact that they love me. No drama, I was not "needed" it was simply for *me.* I actually saved a text message – I used to do this with nice messages all the time – from a Sunshine and Rainbow Friend that reads:

21st January 2016 – Saved Text Message

"No no you're not slack, it's life! I actually miss you so much and can't wait to see you sometime soon! Love you girl, always will 😊"

I'm sure you can imagine what my text before this was? She was right, I wasn't slack, but admittedly, I'd chosen something else over her, something that had (I assume) burnt me out and in complete lethargy, I'd flaked on her.

These were the relationships I was missing out on and when I started to notice this and notice how, if I could choose a different experience, that I could be saved, that I could be 'looked after' and that I could be carried – instead of being the running around-space holder-listener extraordinaire – I started to feel less resentment in my life.

Sunshine and Rainbow Friend

(noun)

A person or friend that makes your soul less hungry.

The moment that I noticed how much I was somewhat sabotaging my life by limiting my Sunshine and Rainbow experiences, was when I started to Walnut without knowing what walnutting was. This is not to say that my drama moments were not fun, I've had a great life, it's been turbulent crazy fun; but my energy always felt empty after, empty and heavy at the same time. I am so grateful to the friends, like the woman who sent me that text, for sticking with me all this time, listening to my shit and unfortunately as much as it is fortunate, letting me treat them, how I was being treated. It is upsetting to admit this and it feels like heavy, ugly guilt and shame. But that's the difference with Sunshine and Rainbow friends, we collect these people for a reason, not just to feed our souls, but because they understand.

Thank you, all flavours of Sunshine and Rainbow friends of the world. It's no doubt, that you are indeed one too, Walnut, we are all a light for someone in the same way our Sunshine and Rainbows are for us. I encourage you to take a moment to reset and re-evaluate if you have this kind of resentment or not and where your Sunshine and Rainbows are on that scale. Then treat yourself, Walnut, because you just opened a door to the insightful internal journey that is, being a Walnut.

For me it was scary to say 'no' at first. You will feel like you are a failure and a disappointment. But like muscle memory, once you walnut and do it a few times, it gets easier – even if you stop for some time, you'll always find your way back to your empowered 'no' and aligned 'yes'. I celebrated it. Every time. Some examples you will find on

Walnut Wednesday the Podcast – one of my very first episodes is called "Saying No" followed by one called "I said YES" – oh, what a journey it has been.

My empowered no's started at first with a little bit of a revenge mindset. You know when you've had all you can take, from no one in particular and you take a type of internal stand with yourself that sounds something like "I'm not going let this happen again!". I was ever so slowly and imperfectly, selecting things to attend by matters of importance such as birthday celebrations versus drinks on a Friday night. I selected having lunch with a Sunshine and Rainbow versus spending a whole evening somewhere else. I prioritised Netflix and Chill. I gave myself Sundays or minimally, Sunday afternoon where possible, to be alone inside my introverted recovery bat cave. I did all this until these little self-decisions became my own personal standard to myself, no one was hurt in the making of this standard, no one was flaked on or double booked and no one needed me so urgently that my self-care bat cave time had to be compromised. I started to ask myself if I'd been living under the guise of some kind of super hero complex (very possible as again, I am a 5/1 profile in Human Design), where my 'shoulds' just ate me alive – why? Why did I *have* to attend this or *should* do that? I know, powerful stuff, right? Most people, Sunshine and Rainbows included, totally understood my way of life. To be honest, they probably didn't even know about it, because it was a pact with myself that I prioritised and worked around. For those that didn't understand, well, most likely it was only a snowball of Bully Demon in my head telling me they didn't or they simply got used to my new personal standard. There was no falling out or sneering looks fuelled by passive aggression. The world didn't end because I'd started setting boundaries for myself and that brought about the ripple effect of my interactions becoming less resentful with the people in my life.

Both Ends of the Boundary Stick

Walnut Wednesday the Podcast episode #62

"It made me feel validated, it made me feel okay to have a boundary and to be frank, I feel like that is how friendships should bloody be!"

In June of 2020 I started to notice that the world began "waking up" and voices that had long since been oppressed began to be acknowledged. The Black Lives Matter movement became so loud and I remember feeling the pressure to use my voice in the discussion of this. I saw the leaders in my online world that I followed, use their voices so powerfully and potently and say the things I felt, which such magnitude that I felt like, as a Walnut, I should too. As a leader in my own way, I wanted so badly to contribute to the movement, the way my mind was speaking and agreeing; however, as if in opposition with my mind, my throat and my voice, have the tendency to mince words and not make much sense. I have always been this way, where I need those close to me to translate what I mean into coherency. The wheel of struggle with my voice is ongoing and Walnut Wednesday continues to turn alongside it, randomly stopping at powerful golden nuggets along the way – sometimes I wonder if it was really me who just said that. During this time, my learned leadership was that I had to learn to speak without speaking and I used my voice powerfully by not using it at all. I used my voice to express that I *struggle* with my voice. I chose not to voice what I so dearly agreed with, passionately, because I knew that I was in a position where my power was not in my words. My power, during that time came from, not following what others were doing, slaying in my lane and coming back to my own truth and in some ways, my reality – some of these coaches had been using their voices with confidence and practiced courage a lot longer than me; they had the social media knowledge to boot. I deeply felt feelings, had thoughts and was in agreeance with what these people were saying about this particular movement; and that, Walnut, *was enough*. This time was pivotal in my growth because I finally gave my lack of a voice, strength. It was always something I hid behind by way of, fearing speaking in groups, choosing not to discuss politics or current affairs, not for fear of being wrong, but for fear of, the meaning of my words being caught up in a fluster and coming out wrong, resulting in my looking like an idiot and 'dumb'.

This for me was a cycle of playing small, playing dumb and feeling constantly frustrated that people thought I was less than. I remember a video recording my that Dad was doing when we were younger, where my cousins, sister and I were sitting in a row – naturally being interviewed and discussing our debut album and latest concert performance (likely in the lounge, the audience consisting of our parents) – and my voice was strong, loud and excited as the hotheaded centre of the group. My Dad then filmed us individually to talk about our performance and the little Lazz in that clip was an entirely different person. Her voice was low, quiet, she'd even developed a lisp in her awkward attempt to speak with her voice all alone. This memory was so early on and add years onto this, it's no wonder I built myself into a person with the story that my voice doesn't matter. Walnut Wednesday The Podcast was a huge catalyst to the voice being expressed in this book today. Past Lazz, the little girl, with the lisp who thought she was nothing on her own, is just as honoured to have you here, inside these pages, as well as Walnut Lazz, gleaming in pride as you witness this entire Walnutting. I want you to know that if I can believe my voice matters, that you can about yours. I see you and I hear you – I'll scream it from the bloody rooftops, Walnut, you are *enough.*

Later, what I used to hide behind from my voice and if I am truly honest, use as a cop out to not do things that make me uncomfortable, looked like the huge snowball fear of confrontation, people pleasing, burnout and yours truly, the frustration that I was made for more but never did anything about it. However, because of the story I was hiding behind, the one I was showing to others and of the story I was making myself believe; I felt like people thought I *was* smaller. I was the meek one who was singled out in meetings with belittling statements like "who would like to present – we won't get Lara to because she has a fear of public speaking". Somewhat patronising, I'm aware – perhaps a story for another day. My point is, Walnut, I had made myself believe something about my voice, that I externalised through my behaviours creating a story that my voice didn't matter and within years, everyone believed it too. I had to start so small to get my power back, to soothe this burn in my belly, this knowing that I *could* do the things. There were very small walnuttings, where I chose to stand in-front of the group to speak a small section of presentation, where I asked for the pen, where I cried in a café because my new truth was that I am meant for so much more, than to feel less than.

Along my Walnut journey a door opened and my voice began to be heard on multiple platforms. An invitation to be a guest on someone else's podcast, followed by another and then followed by being invited to speak in an online summit. A huge change from little Miss Peanut who didn't think her voice mattered to anyone, let alone herself; to a woman whose name was plastered over the internet with some of the influencers she admired most. I watched my live video inside that first summit over and over, shocked at who this Walnut is, what presence I bring to the internet and my mission to change the world flickered before my eyes. I was here… no more toes in the water, I was in for it all; but what now?

I Struggle with my Voice

Walnut Wednesday the Podcast episode #32

"I'm struggling with how to share my voice in this. I feel fear that anything I say is going to come out wrong, because it normally does"

Welcome back Walnut, so you now know that I'd started to implement boundaries, have courageous conversations, use my voice and start to really walnut my way through little things – you also now have an understanding of what a Walnut is, right? But why was I still putting myself down, daily, when it came to how I looked?

Let's talk about the phrase 'Tasty Snack' a term that arose from a podcast interview with Kayla Anderson, one of my favourite self-love gurus of all time! It's a saying I've taken under my wing and now, is almost a life motto, describing me when I am feeling my finest. I've actually been told by a handful of walnuts, that anything to do with tasty snacks reminds my collective of me – I've received 'snack' themed gifts (a bowl that says "tasty snack" and a makeup pallet "sweet and tasty") and am regularly sent snack memes, which I share online!

I think I've failed to mention until now, Walnut, that my weight has slowly crept back up to "the biggest I've ever been" and, I will touch more on this later, because my body image journey, my Snack journey, had been something that morphed its way into Walnut Wednesday as a brand. It started by my using the phrase in jest – I'd post on a social media story 10 seconds of me slapping my belly with the caption "I am a Tasty Snack". I'm sure you can guess it too, Walnut, this was all in fear of being seen - better to be the class clown, right? Than to be hypothetically ridiculed for *actually* liking yourself and admitting that you *do* think you're beautiful… or so my Bully Demon subconsciously once said.

Let me just back track a second. I grew up saying I was fat, not necessarily thinking I was fat, I understood what I categorised as "fat" and I knew that I was not in said category, yet I still bullied myself with the word. I still did not like myself and called myself fat despite my understanding. I genuinely believe it was a fad of the early 2000s – I saw a video about this era, explain that fashion during this time was... hmm... best if you just look it up... fashion was not necessarily about what you were wearing, but the body you hung you're clothes on. Your body was the clothes horse and how thin your arms were and how flat the stomach was, *was* the fashion – because as I remember it, those dresses over jeans... why oh why! The jeans in the 2000's were so low rise that if they didn't sit right, they'd fall of and, God forbid, you have any muffin top! As I mentioned, arms were slim, stomachs (and hair styles) were flat – I remember even pulling my jeans so low to see how far I could get before it wasn't flat anymore, near the bottom of my pelvis – our bodies, our *flat* bodies, were the fashion and If I am honest, I'd be very surprised if I did meet someone from my generation that hasn't had at least one mild aspect of body dysmorphia after coming of age.

So here I am, walnutting my weight back on, no longer with the body of a child, but of a woman who likes to yoyo between clean eating and total gluttony year on year off. As I write, this year being The Year(s) of the Glutton, not to mention what will go down in history as "lockdown weight". I had a real focus on my body and finding the love to give to it – I even called myself a Self-Love Leader at one stage. In my time as being as 'fat the first time I thought I was fat' I never felt good enough to wear a crop top at the gym. It had been something on my life-bucket-list for a very long time (along with scrabble which I have now ticked off too!) and I'd never felt confident enough to do it, despite my waist circumference, my fitness or what I'd had for breakfast. Funny thing, this weight conversation, I think I could write a whole other book on the journey to becoming a Tasty Snack (to be continued...)! I'd seen so many women of different sizes, not just the lean beans, wear little crops to classes and I could never bring myself to do the same. This walnutting was huge for me and I blasted it all over the podcast, my group and on Instagram. A huge learning from this was the cliché "if not now, when?" because I'd denied myself this experience at so many sizes, I didn't see any other way, than simply getting it done; plus, I'd already had evidence from previous walnuttings giving me that feel good factor after the fact, so I knew there would be massive growth in this. On one random day in July of 2020, I got up, I decided to wear that cute little cropped t-shirt I bought in Hawaii and train at the gym – OMG! Naturally, there were obstacles. The gardener was parked behind my car, God forbid I ask him to move! My Mum had the gym swipe card on her key chain and was out – you see, Walnut, just how easy it is to let the excuses build until the simple idea of the walnutting is no more? I am sure you have your own examples of this and the one thing that really helped me get there was exactly that. All I had to do was *get there*, the burn in my belly, the Walnut in me would do the rest.

Wearing a crop top to the gym really set off my body positivity with that simple mindset that if I'd never felt good enough to do it, why not just do it now, with nothing to lose! I stopped using "Tasty Snack" as a joke – which, as I'd mentioned I used to do as a default when I was uncomfortable – where I would wobble my tummy and call myself a snack, almost as a gag; later turned into wobbling my tummy, while at the same time really starting to look at myself, truly stare at my naked body and get my eyes used to what I looked like.

Have you ever realised, Walnut, that we are always covering up? This was a shocking discovery at first and especially when I added Flaptapping my self-love practice, it was quite a confronting process. I know now, that I needed to become this size, to be able to really appreciate my body for how it is and not just how my body looks. For me, loving my body has gone so much deeper than just self-love and self-care, my entire ideology on my worth has changed! So much so that during this time, I was even told I wasn't very memorable (this is also discussed in podcast episode #40 Was that Necessary?) and it didn't bother me like it would have the year prior, because I was already discovering, just how memorable I really am going to be. My reflection after my wearing a crop top workout consisted of multiple car dance parties and the shock that no one looked at me strangely, no one threw up on the floor, no one came up to me and told me I was disgusting. Everyone at the gym was minding their own business, as I was minding mine and pooping my pants inside my own head that *I was wearing a crop top to the gym!*

Let's come back to Flaptapping, I bet you're wondering what it is and how the heck I conjured this crass term up. Again, in a type of jest, I created this however, it's catchy, it has caught on and it is still something I do, maybe not as regular, but still do, to this day! It is a practice where I stand naked in-front of the mirror and tap/wobble all the parts of my body I'm uncomfortable with and say **out loud** "I love you" while simultaneously looking the body parts that move. It has evolved a little over time, but I still do have days where I need to give my Flaboda a loving rub and jiggle, while staring into the mirror. Flaptapping is something that is basically summarised by a form of mirror work – while I wait for the shower to heat up, I stare I myself nude, I wobble the parts of my body that I find offensive at the time, tell the bits "I love you" on repeat – arms, flaboda, side boob, you name it, Walnut, it gets wobbled and loved on. I think the power behind it comes from the act of looking and for years, Walnut, I surrounded myself with friends of all shapes and sizes, but I never stopped to look at myself and at first, it really did give me a fright. Yes, I was buying the bigger sizes but I needed to stop and see what that actually looked like on a naked, not Instagram, no filter level and find a love for it behind the closed bathroom doors first. The idea came to me because I was playing with EFT Tapping at the time, fused with morning affirmations and slapped in some staring at my body, I decided why not somehow combine the three. Now, Walnut, EFT is tapping on particular points of the body, where Flaptapping is simply tapping on the body areas that need extra love - so on a science level, Flaptapping is a little more in the holistic realm. That said, we do have arclines all over our body so it is very likely that you could flaptap your way around these. Either way, it worked for me and I am sure you will or have already, found something that works for you!

I am pleased to say that I didn't just stop at wearing that little t-shirt to the gym. I took it two levels deeper. You know how *underneath* the crop tee that I now wear to the gym, you can sometimes wear a sports bra which can also be worn as a top when at the gym… yeah, those. Well, wearing one of these and only this, outside of the comfort of my own home has been on my life-bucket list too. One sunny day, I was walking along the track near my house (in a crop top!) and it was so hot, I thought to myself 'I wish I could tan right now' which was immediately followed by the walnut inside asking 'why don't you just take it off'. There was no one on that track but I was still mortified inside and again, that burn in my belly, that knowing, scarecited feeling of a walnutting brewing its way to full flavour was bubbling right up and over me. With a flash, my crop top was off and I was walking along my local track in a different kind of crop, a smaller bra, on trend crop, that I thought only a certain type of person was "allowed" to wear. Hah! Look at me soar! It wasn't long and after I passed a few people on my walk where again, no one looked at me strangely, no one threw up on the track, no one came up to me and told me I was disgusting. Everyone walking was minding their own business, as I was minding mine and pooping my pants inside my own head that *I was wearing a crop top outside!*

This feeling felt familiar, almost comfortable - a couple years of walnutting you will soon feel this way, Walnut, don't worry! So that same day, I took it up a notch. I still had to take my walk off of the track and into the local village to pick something up. In my mind, I was going to put the crop back on (which was still a walnutting in itself, wearing *that* through the village), but something stopped me. I heard my Sacral, the burn in my belly once more saying 'just do it and see what happens' my little line one Investigator in full force. I'd worked my mind into such a frenzy wondering what *could* happen that in the blink of an eye I was on the concrete footpath just moments away from the shop I needed to enter – WEARING A CROPPED SPORTS BRA! Again, no one looked at me strangely, no one threw up on the floor, no one came up to me and told me I was disgusting. In fact, the woman at the counter looked at me as if this was my *normal* get up! She didn't even glance down at my flaboda, at my rolls or any of my side boob – she simply asked "have you just been out for a run? It's such a lovely day" *mind blowing brains emoji* WHAT THE HECK?! As I write this book, this moment is one of my favourite walnuttings to date and one of my biggest personal achievements. I still remember this moment fondly and I will never forget it – as I pierced her eyes with my glare just waiting for her to look down at my body and she didn't. I'd never felt such a personal sense of accomplishment as I did that day and I hope, Walnut, that you find or have already, found yours. If this chapter resonates with you, I encourage you to look at yourself. Ask yourself what your "crop top moment" is and if it's not time to walnut about it, ask yourself why.

What's your Crop Top?

Walnut Wednesday the Podcast episode #36

"Walnuttings are just singular moments and that's all it takes!"

Walnut, we've touched on my physical environment and my emotional state(s), however, like a set of train tracks, my spiritual environment was running alongside these places, these walnuttings, as well as contributing to them.

I want to take you back through two spiritual practices that have been a part of not only my growth, but a part of the umbrella that is Walnut Wednesday. Let's back track all the way back into unworthiness, overworking and consistently subconsciously seeking validation in every single 'should do' or 'have to' resulting in total burnout. The year is 2018 and before I even had the faintest idea what a Walnut was - other than a literal source of protein - where I made my first investment in myself. I label this one my first, where it wasn't really *the* first, because while it was a certification, it was more on the esoteric side to qualifying for something rather than your typical degree (I do have one of those too) or certificate in your typical thing - I enrolled to participate in a Reiki Level 1 certification.

Now, Walnut, it may have been my line 5 and my undeniable superhero complex, but I've always felt somewhat called to and aligned with, the word "healer" - the word actually channelled in again later in a meditation at a group workshop I attended. I remember my friend looked at me like "wow" when the host asked me what word came through for me – I always have been and still am deeply connected with tingles in my hands and with energy. Funny side note: I always know if I am getting sick because I wake up with a sort of numb, pins and needles from my hands to my forearms! I've always felt things in a profound way, I'm highly empathic and, when not in the best alignment, well... as I mentioned, unworthiness, overworking and consistently subconsciously seeking validation and burnout creep into focus.

So, I'm there, deep inside the frustrations of people pleasing, eating everyone's shit and feeling like a doormat; while simultaneously I was resonating with healing, psychic-ness and my ever-longing closet obsession for witchcraft. My friend, who at the time was going through a trauma of her own and was, if you will, "coming out of the spiritual closet" – things were so different back then in regard to being the "woke" we all know post the year 2020 – and she mentioned to me that she'd found a teacher, she'd enrolled in a Reiki certification and that knowing I was "in to that stuff" suggested I join her. Walnut, this was a time for me where I resonated with not having money; despite paying my rent, paying for transport and eating three meals (plus snacks...) a day, I still identified with the story lack. There were so many layers to this, Walnut, most of which all circle back to the worthiness and people pleasing piece that I have repeated throughout this book. Being invited to join my friend in this certification was one of the first times, I made something work financially for me and my sacral alone. When I first responded "I can't, I have no money" to make this investment, it felt, not good enough and I knew this was something I needed to do – thank you credit card gods! I felt like I needed another sign (habits of justification are a whole other ball game) so I ended up calling this teacher and expressing my interest.

I explained that I felt called to this certification but that I didn't know what to do or how I could validate this investment and she even waived the credit card fee for me. I still believe to this day that she knew Reiki was calling to me and my Sacral knew it all the time. It simply was not good enough, for my soul at that time, to use not having enough money as my cop out on this purchase on myself, no way.

I remember sitting at the dinner table telling my family that I had made this investment. An amount that now, seems like peanuts (hehe – get it), felt like all the money in the world – Bully Demon was coming in hot asking me if I was sure that this was the right thing to do. I was somewhat interrogated about what it means, how could I possibly heal someone by being near them and understanding what a chakra is. The funny thing was, Walnut, that I knew it all along, because *I'd been doing it all along*, Reiki simply gave me a modality to make it linear. I've always felt like a lighthouse, I've always felt called to the word "healer" and I've always known inside of me is some kind of magic – albeit covered in a world of conditioning and societal shit that I've been trudging through on this Walnut journey of mine.

Reiki found me and called me in. I remember stepping into my certification whole heartedly and after my attunement the oracle cards that came out for me were "Faith in the Process", the Ascended Master Merlin's "Healing Energy" and the action card "you know what to do" – I was home, in a strange esoteric home and I knew that this had simultaneously started to work through me, paving the way for Walnut Wednesday to be born in the years to follow.

Universal Exchanges

Walnut Wednesday the Podcast episode #25

"Learning Reiki really helped me to become a channel and still be able to help people; but be able to let that go at the end"

It wasn't long after Walnut Wednesday started to feel like my natural way forward that I felt called to respond to a post online and stepped in another type of exchange. This was for a side role that really opened the doors to the umbrella that is Walnut Wednesday – poof! Goes the umbrella – a Virtual Assistant, assisting my favourite person online in exchange for payment. Alongside Reiki healings, this job has been a main source of my brand's income and it was time for me to step into a new way of leadership and taking myself seriously as business lady! I started to truly identify with the word 'leader' - I felt like I was officially running a business and with it came a new kind of emotional intelligence, where I was not just thinking about an emotion at that time or an excuse when I'd done something wrong.

This portion in my life brought about new learnings of ways to ask questions and make mistakes with integrity in a new role and not letting it fester. I started to take on obstacles with truth and with total honestly. I began learning so much about what goes on behind the scenes for online entrepreneurs that I've felt nothing but insanely blessed to work for one of my favourite coaches on the planet.

It was interesting to note that accepting add additional role, I also looked at all of the transactions I'd made on myself up to that point and started to focus on the investments I'd made in *me*. The things that you spend on but have nothing physical to show for it like personal development and sometimes, travel. I noticed my worth and how much emotional intelligence I'd learned, since I'd started my journey and since I decided I was a Walnut. I was leading, I was learning and I for once in my life, felt worthy. I'd invested OVER FIVE THOUSAND New Zealand dollars in group programs, readings and healings at this point and it didn't even scare me – quite a sum for someone who was afraid of spending a mere $200 on a Reiki certification right? Some of the things I was not necessarily investing money in either, some classes that I regularly took were free ones, where the only investment was time – one of my manifestation and money teachers, Kate Decker, says "if you desire it, it must be available" – there will always be a way for you to do the thing if you want to. I think we make money mean so much, however, like us and like manifesting things, it is the energy that we are putting into it. Think about it Walnut, humans used to trade live stock for grains or vice versa, it was only one day that someone decided a piece of paper would mean something and thus, money was created (disclaimer I have no sources for this statement and sort of made it up – but you get the picture).

Having money to be able to invest in myself was great however I'm trying to explain that it wasn't ever money that was the issue and I had to spend at-least $5000 in my currency to actually understand what that meant. Walnut, tell me if you've ever had a friend or knew someone, on a similar salary to you, yet you had "no money" and they were always buying new makeup or going on little trips or simply, always seemed to have a dollar to spend? Well, this was me too and I always felt like "the poor friend". However, I was not "poor". I had money, it was simply being prioritised in different places –

namely my relationship and our large annual holidays we would take, where we'd spend the year paying it off until the next one. My priority was different and this is easy to say looking back but back then I always felt like I was left behind – I wonder now, if that is what others felt when I would take my holidays? What I am getting at Walnut, is that I was living in lack and I was in a sense taking these big purchases for granted because I was not seeing their worth – rather, because I could not physically see personal growth and development, I had nothing to materialistically show.

I could talk about money a lot longer Walnut, but what I wanted to explain in this section was more in the exchanges I was making and how these were transmuting on the inside, while at the same time, how much the limiting stories I affirmed, such as "I'm the poor friend" were adding further layers onto my progress, sitting dormant and heavy on my self-worth until the shedding would start. I give a lot of my energy in a lot of different places, Walnut. My energy being money, time, healings, however, now I see that where I have or haven't *invested* my energy in the past has been able to help me unlock some of those layers and in turn feel brave enough to be super transparent with where my energy goes; and I wouldn't change anything I've done in the past because of what I've learned and how I feel now. Our inner stories are so powerful and I think the most interesting part about being a Walnut, is noticing exactly what those stories are – you may literally hear them either in your head or how you automatically respond, you may think them after something happens – and there are so many different ways that they can be a detriment to our happiness over time. I chose to celebrate noticing and when I noticed, it would mean I'd be opened a door to where another walnutting was waiting around the corner and Future Lazz, having one less thing to deal with later, was waiting around the next.

Transforming in the Transaction

Walnut Wednesday the Podcast episode #37

"For the first time ever, I am not embarrassed to tell you that I invested in myself. I am worth it. I'm so worth it"

When I got to a stage of semi-comfort with my voice – and that's not to say I could magically talk in-front of large groups, but rather, my podcast episodes went from heavily prepared notes and uptight effort, to an unexpected sense of unorganised flow. I began to make my conversations, genuine conversations because something that I'd learned along the way was to play to my strengths and my strength was that I undoubtedly will always prefer "progress over perfection" as my friend Jamie would always say. I'll always rather have started, sometimes even finished, something over slaving over the something for days because it is not good enough – so I decided to no longer stress about the expression of my voice and talking notes that were always word for word. I had a platform, I'd been practicing my voice and I'd been interviewing some pretty damn inspiring people; all of whom, use their voices in ways that I admire. So, what's to say, I couldn't use my platform and my voice in collaboration with theirs?

This was a strange concept at first and I first looked to Kate, who you will remember from every ten episodes of Walnut Wednesday the podcast, where we communicate in this unscripted conversation style anyway (if you're a podcast listener, Walnut, you'll know that every ten episodes are basically, as if you were a fly on the wall, recorded conversations between Kate and I – we talk like this offline too!). This was a perfect way to up-level how I use my voice and a great test came from a hot topic that had been brewing within me. Again, I felt passionate, I agreed with some of the things I had heard, however, the word mincing thing story I'd created kept coming up again and again. I really wanted to share about a topic that had been coming up in multiple areas of my life – all areas in fact – physically, when I was walking around, spiritually, in the sisterhood wounding and womb healing I'd been look at and emotionally, where I started to investigate *why* I didn't want to take up space. If you have a moment, Walnut, check out Walnut Wednesday the podcast: Episode #80 *Feminist? An Honest Conversation* and see if you notice some of those things listed above.

That's the thing when you have 'a Kate' in your life, a friend who will not only challenge your thinking, but also be able to understand what you mean through active listening and, sometimes, finish your sentences. The art of using my voice in collaboration was in effect! Going forward, I understood, that my magic, my power doesn't have to come from what I *specifically* say and particularly, as lonely as the Walnut journey can feel, that I am *never* truly alone – all I have to do is ask!

Collaboration to use My Voice

Walnut Wednesday the Podcast episode #81

"It's a stepping stone into how I want to use my words or how I want to express myself, via collaborating with somebody else - because you *choose* who you want to use words with"

With this innovative sense of worthiness, leadership and this new found a confidence with my voice, I felt another pull to start voicing what it felt like for me, to be a "survivor of being left behind" and I wanted to start using my voice about suicide prevention, discuss my story and how I felt. I was in a time, where I'd had enough practice in getting vulnerable that I felt really inspired to plant the seeds of my heaviness, to showcase reality for so many of us and what survival of grief and loss means for me. I wanted to share what how to "keep on", really means for me.

A key thing to note through this book, Walnut, is that I was recording a releasing one episode a week the whole way through. I've never and still, to this day have not, missed a single Walnut Wednesday podcast episode since it aired in November 2019 and you will see - rather, you will hear - scattered throughout the collection of episodes are walnuttings where I often come back to this topic and new stages of my journey of loss. There are episodes which I've not been able to re-listen to, in particular Episode #41 *The Elephant in the Room(s)* which I'd mentioned earlier in this book. There are some very key moments throughout my journey that you have been privy too solely by just being here and of course with that, you learn alongside me, as I share new walnuttings each week – how situations made me feel, what I did or didn't do, no matter how "big" or small the *thing* really is.

Sometimes, Walnut, and especially when it comes to loss, the smallest thing, for me in particular has triggered almost a trauma response, where everything I've ever felt, backdating to the day of knowing about the person's death flood back in an instant. I've share with you podcast episodes about simply moving a jacket from under my pillow to the wardrobe and even an episode of accidentally deleting a photo I will never get back. These episodes are all about how hard these moments were and what I learned, my moments of brave - my walnuttings. I imagine there will be more too - it sounds silly doesn't it, the breaking of your heart over moving some clothing or deleting a photo, but what if they were of your last connection to your person?

The below section mentions suicide please do not feel pressured to read this chapter and skip ahead if you need to

A story about a client that came in to my former work where a year prior, at a different store she'd booked a trip and had come back to me with that same quote to re-book the entire thing again. English was not her first language, she seemed very overexcited and out of the blue in a blaze' way explained that "when I was last there, I was going to kill myself" which, after the experiences close to my heart, really made my stomach drop. She'd mentioned that she wanted to visit a cave where a group of young children had died, explaining that it was all about her book she was writing, all the while continuing to mention "kill myself", "I tried to kill myself", every sentence just stabbing me in the gut as I tried to compartmentalise! Naturally, I didn't book this holiday on the spot (like you are encouraged to do in sales where possible), because I was feeling very triggered, uncomfortable, *kill myself, I tried to kill myself* so I created a quote for her to think about and made an appointment to follow up. This interaction really sat with me, heavily, *kill myself, I tried to kill myself* for the rest of the day and as I do with many of life's queries, I checked in with my Dad about it. He mentioned how horrible I would feel if something ever did happen to this woman and I never did anything about it, so the next day for her appointment I walnutted. I'd printed a list of numbers and health lines and placed the page inside an envelope. I explained to her that after our conversation, I felt incredibly deeply about it, that I never want her to feel this way again *kill myself, I tried to kill myself* and that if she wanted, I had this envelope with some numbers if she ever needed someone to talk to *kill myself kill myself* and that there was no pressure to take it if she didn't want to. She gratefully took the envelope that I handed over to her with a shaky hand and a crackling voice. It was incredibly hard to address the that fact that she had tried to kill herself, it was incredibly hard to offer something in exchange for that information, advice or 'assistance' but I felt much lighter after I did. We booked her trip, she paid in full and I did not hear from her for a while.

On a random day following this, in the lead up to her trip, she came into my office with tears streaming down her face. She explained that her doctor – at this point I felt a relief at the mention of this – had advised she was not fit to fly and should cancel this trip. This woman was the complete opposite of the high energy, erratic, excitable woman that came in to book the initial trip. She was absolutely devastated and broken. On the technical side, the refunding and cancellations were done and with a heavy heart we arranged to get as much money back as possible for the booking (some things were unfortunately non-refundable). A year or so later, my having left and moved on and away, I received a message from my former Team Leader and still my friend, who said that a former client had remembered me and left something for me. During the booking process we did discuss that we both spoke German and what she'd left for me was a manuscript of her poetry, some from years ago and some more recent. Some of the poems are in English and others in German. On the front of the cover, it reads (translated from German) "For Lara, you are an angel" which hit my soul so deeply.

I tell this story, Walnut, because the process of meeting this woman, from beginning to end, even receiving this heart-warming gift from her, because it did, like moments I've shared, bring everything that I have been through, right back to the surface of my heart. I tell you this story, because I – and I do suspect like you in some ways, Walnut – identify as someone who has been "left behind" from suicide and someone who is going through the motions of surviving after death, not necessarily my own. I wanted to start using the strength I'd found in practicing my voice to talk about this more, because no one teaches you how to deal with grief or how to survive after someone is gone. In my opinion, no one tells you how to constructively offer help if someone says something like this woman did or even, how to ask for help. No one necessarily tells you what the best way to not-trigger someone or to not-trigger yourself is and while I don't know either, I think that starting a conversation around this and by simply being brave enough to be vulnerable, it can somehow be made to be normal to admit that it is a bad day, rather than soldier on and pretend it is. How many times when someone asks you how you are do you just say "good" – is it actually? Notice responses like "not too bad" and are you actually feeling bad or just dimming down feeling great? I genuinely believe that practicing my voice, using it to share walnuttings and be brave, is a start to a more open dialogue, which by default, is the start to actually enjoying who you are – because you won't have yourself to hide behind and be ashamed of. That is my truth in Walnut Wednesday and it only takes that little baby step, even once a week, to start the journey and join me!

Hey, Walnut, you've got this!

Moving Along

Walnut Wednesday the Podcast episode #09

"This is me letting my 'Jack" go; shedding guild, shedding pain and deciding what I want to keep"

I came to a point in my journey where I had three jobs: my 9-5, my Virtual Assistant role and Walnut Wednesday, not just a podcast but *a business*, MY real life, very own business! What a strange thing to be able to get my head around – and a walnutting in itself at that.

I want to share my experience during the time where the security of my call centre job, the one that "saved me" from my old life of unworthiness, was coming to a close via contract end. It was an uncertain time of high stress, a lot of waiting and, with my new found worthiness, I also realised the shift work, after eight months, did not suit the lifestyle I desired anymore. Despite this, I was grateful for the time I'd spent here. I not only had my out of the time in my life that no longer served me, I actually needed to trial shift work; in fact, it even felt aligned and worked really well for me for a huge portion of that time - it gave me so much more time to put into Walnut Wednesday! It gave me time to go outside, to learn flow and to explore the aspect of having ease in my life – rather than burning myself out for little to no reward and, to spite my self-worth.

During this time, I was also exploring self-validation because it was a time where I was applying and interviewing for new jobs. This of course, brought back to the surface old feelings of not being good enough with a side of self-doubt – naturally, due to the rejections and "unsuccessful" emails and letters I received. Despite how much emotional intelligence I'd gained and how much I treated the interviews as experiments, I knew that somewhere in my body, I was feeling deflated and adding this to the stress that I was storing into my subconscious. I learned two key tips during this time, the first being not to wear a full face of makeup – for no reason other than to be realistic and not set expectations that I will wear a full face of makeup to this new potential job - uh hello, this isn't a wild night of debauchery! - and the second was to write notes. I don't know how many times I've psyched myself out in an interview trying to act naturally, while at the same time trying to memorise all my great examples, only to catch a blank and look like a deer in the headlights! Notes were key throughout this experience, completely owning it, acknowledging that I brought them at prompts and *not* feeling bad or rather, embarrassed if I had to read off of them due to nerves; and you know what, Walnut? *No one cared*! Again and again, I build evidence that the things I think are the end of the world (like wearing a crop top to the gym or a sports bra through the village and, in this case, reading off of my notes in an interview), prove to be so minute that, even I myself don't seem to care at times. I mean that in the most positive way, Walnut. Sometimes things snowball so huge in our minds, where Bully Demon will let us balloon a concept up to epic negative proportions, when in reality, once we do it, once we Walnut, we simply plant these courageous seeds of quick confidence and in the blink of an eye you're a few baby steps forward with some walnuttings under your belt to boot! Now I know what you're thinking, "easier said than done, Lazz", I know, I've said and sometimes still do this to myself! However, I've found the key for me has always been about Future Lazz. A lot of people talk about their Future Self or their Higher Self and for me, aspects of this are true, but full transparency here... for me it's out of laziness, rather than any love and light spiel. Let me explain; do you always see on social media, particularly in sales, sometimes even coaches, telling you how much you need the thing because when you're done or when you have it, you will get XYZ, right? For me, it's always sounded something like, "Lazz, if you do this now, you won't have to do it later" – plain and simple Walnut! I am the type of gal who will buy the nuts in bulk, be broke for two weeks, just because I know, for three more months I won't have to buy extra nuts! (I don't know where the nut analogy came from – it must be all this Walnut talk!). If you put in the walnutting now, the more you can sit back and relax later, right? If you are courageous now, you will reap the rewards from the lessons learnt later. If you are brave now, you will shit-your-pants-possibly-have-a-panic-attack and then feel accomplished after. You don't need the thing, you don't need anything outside of yourself, Walnut; and for me, starting small in honour of lazy Future Lazz was key.

I was due to go on a family holiday near the end of 2020 and before I left, I had one last job interview. Now this was the one where I'd really had it. I'd had enough of interviewing for experience, I'd had enough of talking myself up and repeating the same hypothetical situations that you never actually know how you will respond until you're in the hypothetical role. I actually had an anxiety attack catching the train into the city because I could not even bother to give myself the optimistic speech of something like "if anything, Lazz it's a great experience" – you know that pleasant little back up saying you give yourself just in-case of emergency purposes? I thought "my (work)life isn't great but it's fine" because my call centre contract was in progress and it was a short walk from home - all the excuses under the sun to settle for something that wasn't right for me (again – funny how history repeated itself but in a much shorter amount of time, here). Long story short, Walnut, I showed up to the interview, little to no makeup and using notes (the two hacks I have now gifted you with – you're welcome) and when I met my boss, I just knew I wanted to work for her, the vibe was high! I met a friend for lunch afterwards and not even two hours after the interview, I got a phone call asking if I'd be interested in what was initially the hypothetical role - so I guessed my boss wanted me on her team too! In true Walnut fashion, I celebrated that I was made to feel validated, successful and felt the tension melt away from my shoulders. I could now go on my family holiday and fully recharge because, well, because I walnutted!

Mindset Can Be Externalised

Walnut Wednesday the Podcast episode #77

"I ended up doing little small baby steps, to make myself, to put myself out there. It does stem from being honest with yourself, I had to really be intentional with myself and notice"

Another pivotal moment - though, I'm going to suggest that there will be more, just not throughout this book - was respectfully declining to speak in a summit right before I went away. I could feel in my whole body, that it simply didn't feel right to say yes.

Up until that point my Walnut-life-balance was really not at its finest and I hadn't quite figured out where my Walnut life ended and home life began – these were new boundaries that I hadn't played with yet. I was in a place where this holiday was my break away, my celebration for the year I'd had and the calm before the storm of my first ever online festival, where everything was already organised. All I had left to do was to be there when the speakers showed up. My main reason for declining was that the dates were *during* that holiday where I'd have had to speak and I'd made a promise of "no work" to my Jordy and my family – which felt really good when I thought about it long enough! (Old habits die hard) It was strange to say no, to something where I had the energetic capacity to do the thing, but it was with further ease I was able to think about my trip *by* saying no, because I had no obligation to be anywhere at any time – yes, it was strange to have something so stress-free. I actually ended up pre-recording something for the host to post while I was away, which was something fresh and new – another walnutting under my ever-extending belt of bravery. Pre-recording was a new learning and it was interesting to note that I was still nervous, despite it being recorded. It was like a whole new set of nerves but it still felt really good to be able to pre-be there in that summit, knowing I could enjoy myself on my break whole heartedly.

Walnutfest 2020, my first online festival, which I believe to this day, is one of the best things I've ever seen on the internet (but I'm biased, right?). Before we finish this chapter and potentially, this book, I'd like to talk to you, Walnut, about who I stepped into becoming from hosting Walnutfest. Walnut, I cannot even put into words how much fun I had creating this festival. I'd asked almost all of my favorite people on the internet if they would visit my group and do a training for my audience. These women were coaches, teachers, business owners, all people who I'd collaborated with or bought programs from for that year. This festival was to celebrate Walnut Wednesday being one year old - what a huge milestone for a peanut identifying Walnut who didn't think she could be anything, right? One key moment in preparation of this, Walnut, was *to ask*. I had to walnut, be brave and invite the speakers. It's a bit like when we talked about parents and family becoming "just people" where the mentors I was (and still do) following online are also that. They are, we are all, *just people.* I think the pedestal putting is quite a – albeit natural – human matter where we subconsciously deem ourselves less than because of comparison. I had to really look this in the eye and, like wearing the crop top, I asked myself "why not? - if not now when?". What was the harm right? I'd been to many summits and by then, I'd also spoken as a guest in a handful myself, why was it not my turn to create an epic potion of collaboration and training for *my collective*, for my followers, for my Walnut Tree? Of course, Walnut, so she did… and it was one of the biggest online festivals I'd personally ever seen, with the most powerful line up of speakers – twenty including myself! I held space for nineteen high level boss ass bananas to speak in MY damn group and the twentieth was ME!

The thing that really got me so emotional for Walnutfest was that the people that presented, that said yes to being in my festival, were all people I look up to and people that inspire me; so, the fact they were inside my festival to celebrate my business, using my name, knowing who I am - wow. It was like the ultimate fan girl experience apart from *I was facilitating the* experience – I was like organiser of the band on tour, where they all give special thanks to their managers at the end of gigs. I wasn't just a little peanut spectating on their live streams anymore, I wasn't just looking up at them and their power wishing I could do the same. For the first time in my life, Walnut, I felt like an equal to some of the people I look up to the most – I wasn't the girl at the concert who'd been there, watched got the t-shirt and left. I wasn't just the waitress collecting glasses, I WAS AT THE DAMN PARTY IN ATTENDANCE!

Walnut, what I learned in this time is that you can have pleasure without excess stress. Sometimes we come to situations in such divine timing but we do not quite know it until after. In hindsight the situation will look like it was a strategic game of chess where each move was designed by angels with only you living your best life in mind - it's mad! How are you listening to your intuition and following nudges like this, Walnut? Have you experienced something like this before? And if you've not, where can you get quiet enough to recharge and do it?

Walnutfest 2020

Walnut Wednesday the Podcast episode #63

"I am not longer at the show in the cheap seats watching these women perform. I'm literally at the party *with them* - I have levelled up to this level and it's a privilege. It's a testament to walnutting and being brave"

I look back on the musings of this book after time between these walnuttings have passed and I am in complete awe of myself, of you, of us. There are walnuttings inside this book, moments where, looking back I don't even feel scarecited and some of these habits are now simply a part of my life as I know it.

Look at where we are, Walnut. How many baby steps and 'bits of brave' has it taken us to get to this exact moment, right here right now. One day you'll be looking back, much like you are now and asking yourself "how the hell did I make it" what specifically did it take. Then without a shadow of a doubt, you'll look within yourself deeply and you'll think "it wasn't the oracle cards, the healings, the courses. It wasn't the advice I took or the expensive things" – and knowing that while all these things aided you in getting perspective and kept life interesting and enjoyable – you'll come to the conclusion that "it was because of *me*" because you'll realise that you've been a Walnut, walnutting all along. I know you will feel this, Walnut, because I have felt it myself. Lara Marie Gieseke, the girl making debut performances swinging from an apple tree. The young girl translating German to English to German on bike rides with her Opa Karl. The girl who somewhere along the way picked up that she would never be good enough. The girl who thought she was fat, ugly and not worth a second glance. The girl who lost many times, that grieved and wallowed in apathy and darkness. The girl who invested over one thousand New Zealand dollars to join an eight-week business program with no idea why. The girl who started a podcast for no other reason than a universal butt smack, gut feeling, sacral urge to do so. This girl walnutted her way into a woman she is proud of.

I want to share a poem with you that I wrote in a dark time on my Walnut journey which I have not shared anywhere other than the container in which it was created. I'm sharing this with you, Walnut, because I want you to feel, through me, what it feels like to rise and to morph from a Peanut into a Walnut from the inside out; and I want you know, if you don't already, what you *are* already capable of.

19 February 2021 - Post inside Wild Woman
(a group program by Viola Hug)

I am not who you think I am.

You think I am kind,
Therefore you think me weak,
You think I am rooted here,
Therefore I can be walked across.

I am not who you think I am.

I am not here to save you,
I am not here to eat your lies,
To clean your mess,
I am not delicate.

I am not who you think I am.

I am hellfire when scorned.
My power is from within.
I am a Rising Phoenix.
My power is from within.

I am infinite.
I am immeasurable.
You underestimate me.

I am not who you think I am.

I put Period Blood on my Face

Walnut Wednesday the Podcast episode #93

"It invoked this primal feeling of strength"

You made it to this page for a reason – I made it to *writing this page* for a reason. We are forever tethered together by one, small, sometimes unseen thread. We are bonded because we are both the Walnut. We are both the person that decided and decides to be brave.

So much has changed since Walnut Wednesday the podcast was born, yet so much remains the same. I have witnessed my own personal evolution from Peanut Girl to Walnut Woman. I have conquered my own obstacles, had tough conversations, I've been in situations on all points various of the scale, big or small. I've felt all the feelings under the sun, sometimes in complete polarity. I've shared, I've lost and I've spent a whooole lot of money. I did it all, the same way I am *doing* it all now; a baby step, a 'butt smack', a small download hidden inside a moment; a moment to steer me down the path of a new idea, divinely planted for me, actioned *by me*. Every instance, every moment becomes something new, scareciting - but the one thing remains constant and that one thing is all it takes... one Walnutting a week.

A parting message

from my Reiki teacher after my Level 1 attunement

"Confidence is not 'will they like me'
Confidence is 'I'll be fine if they don't'"

I'm going to end this story where I am at now. It has been almost a year and many words later since I decided to share them in the form of a book. I'm in my monster giant "expensive", super king size bed, inside my own first home, Nana the Labrador (my 'sister') is snoozing on Jordan's side of the bed. The Fat Birds are chirping outside, I do not live far from their nest. I took a week off, to nurse myself back from burnout. My only task for this week is to tell you some of my story and as the pages in this slice of my journey come to an end, I welcome you to begin yours. I can hear a faint humming, unsure if it is a neighbour singing to her children, or music, or the hum of my own soul acknowledging the closing of this book. My first book.

Let it be known, Walnut, that this book was written for no reason other than, because I wanted to. When I thought about writing and publishing something, I felt scarecited and I moved – because, well, why not? As you know by now, I feel things on an incredibly deep level and my mind constantly races a million miles an hour. This book is but only *a piece* of my expression. My vulnerable expression, giving you a chance to see a snip of life through my lens. The funny thing is, Walnut, that I don't know where to end this book because *being a Walnut is infinite*. Every single week I share a new learning with you and every single week I walnut in some capacity;
and ***that is enough.***

Origins of Walnut Wednesday

Walnut Wednesday the Podcast episode #01

"Walnut means growth, expansion, courage, bravery, kindness, affection - all on a personal level"

Walnut Wednesday the podcast was born on the first Wednesday of November 2019.

The podcast is a journey created to inspire Walnuts to feel confident & love themselves by being a Walnut [noun] a person that decides to be brave.

Connect @walnutwednesday across all social media and at **www.walnutwednesday.com**

www.ingramcontent.com/pod-product-compliance
Ingram Content Group UK Ltd.
Pitfield, Milton Keynes, MK11 3LW, UK
UKHW042015190726
13854UKWH00005B/2296